What People Think of Me

Your Quick Guide to Caring Less

By

Benjamin Kennet

What People Think of Me

Copyright © 2017

ISBN: 9781520260549

Warning and Disclaimer

Publisher Contact

Skinny Bottle Publishing

books@skinnybottle.com

Introduction

At some point, we all wonder what others think of us. For some, it is a fleeting thought that lingers less than the time it takes a hummingbird's heart to beat. Still, there are some of us that spend an ample amount of time consumed with that seemingly never ending pulse of a question drumming through the mind: What do others think of me?

Anybody that has ever been there knows that it isn't a fun place to be. It's self-crippling and in the end, there is no use. But still, we put ourselves through this mental torture. Where do we hope this will lead? Are we trying to please everyone? Are we simply egomaniacs that have the sentient feelings that everyone else out there has their eyes on us? Of course we are not.

Self-questioning is bound to happen. Especially if you're new on the scene wherever you are. It could be the classroom, the workplace, or a different city. You can even move across town and feel that overwhelming pressure of wondering what others think as you have an entirely different group of neighbors to meet.

Staying inside in dire self-isolation is certainly no life for anybody. But don't think that being self-conscious is a bad thing that needs to be corrected. If it limits your ability and your comfort at interacting with the world then you may want to consider some exercises to help you overcome this. However, being socially conscious, if not exaggerated, is absolutely healthy. In fact, it is necessary.

Approval is something that can be a healthy motivator when you combine it with your virtues. Mixed in with self-determination, integrity, and confidence, the act of seeking approval is less of a crutch and more of a driving force that helps make a person the best they can be.

However, this need for approval can also be a way to define ourselves, and consequentially limit ourselves from experiencing richer lives, closer and more in tune with our true dreams. Have you ever stuck around somewhere you didn't want to be just because you were worried what other people would think of you if you left? Or even worse, have you ever stuck around somewhere (think job) just because you didn't think you were good enough to get out there and find something better.

See how this sense of approval can get in the way of achieving your dreams if you let it? So how do you find a balance? Well, there is little balance. It is sort of one of those things where you have to put the opinions of others up on the shelf where they belong. You can look at them. Take them into consideration if you want, but ultimately they are not close to you. Unless you have a crystal ball and know how to use it, you probably don't really know what others are thinking anyhow. In other words, we just never truly know what somebody else thinks of us. You can even ask them directly and you still aren't guaranteed a direct answer. Why is this? Most of the time people might not be too forthcoming because they are wrapped up in their own world of seeking approval. Yep. You're not alone. Most people are actively trying to do their best to fit in with mainstream and let's face it, nobody really likes mean people.

So how do you get to find out what others think about you? There are some ways that you can go about it, that make it a little easier for someone to give their honest opinion without running the risk of looking like a complete jerk. You could hold an anonymous survey I suppose. But really? If it matters so much to you then you really need to take a cold hard look in the mirror and ask yourself, why that is.

There's no judgment here. It's not a bad thing, but if you are really thinking so much about what others think of you then you are spending a lot of time wrapped up in worrying and overthinking. There is a whole world out there to go and explore right from your front door. And if you did know what others thought of you, what would you do then? Would you change to fit into their every whim and wish? Would you become angry if you knew that they didn't think as highly of you as you expected? How would you handle the news that you aren't the center of their world?

This is not to sound cold, but it's just one of those facts of life. People spend far more time thinking about themselves than they do thinking about somebody else. Most people go through their day focused on the tasks that they have at hand, what they have to do later in the day, and what comes next. There is way too much going on for the average person that keeps them from thinking about you. Somebody might see something they admire or dislike in a person but the thought really only lingers for a millisecond. It doesn't resonate.

If you are worried or concerned about how you appear or behave around other people, then you quite possibly might already have a clue as to how you want to perceived. All you can do then is do your best to uphold that image and maintain it. Some people may get it, but don't be surprised if most people don't even notice. It's simply because they are too busy focused on their own lives. All you can do is focus on making yourself happy and being comfortable in your own skin.

Why Doesn't Anyone Like Me?

If you ever have had the feeling that no matter where you go nobody likes you then you are no different than the rest of us. Sure there are some people out there that will tell you that they don't care what other people think, but these are usually the individuals that are doing everything they can to make sure that other people are seeing them the exact way they want to be seen. There is nothing to be ashamed of in thinking that nobody likes you.

If you are like me then you have been down that isolation hallway of life before. You know the one. It's where it seems like everyone is talking under their breath at you. Nobody bothers to say hi back to you, and if they do acknowledge your presence it's only with some sort of awkward gaze like they are looking at an alien species that has been rounded up in the latest freak show.

For the longest time, I just dove right into the stares. I did everything I could to make them look at me like I was more of a freak. I figured if they weren't going to like me then I was going to do the best I could to make sure that the reason they didn't was because of me and not because of them. This of course, as I see now, was completely arrogant of me. I was wasting my life still trying to make peace with the fact that I lacked social skills.

It wasn't like I was aware of this. I knew I was different but I had no idea that the people around me would have been there for me, had I not been so self-centered. I'm not suggesting that you are self-centered, at least not in a bad way. What helped me get over it was to stop thinking about why nobody liked me, and start thinking about reasons why they should.

Be a Friend, Make a Friend

Was I doing anything to be a friend to anybody? I wasn't listening, I wasn't paying attention, I wasn't there for others when they were hurting and just needed a shoulder to cry on. It was no wonder that I was suddenly isolated and alone. Truly alone. This doesn't have to be you, though. And if it is already, you need to know that you are not alone. Whoever you are out there, you are not alone.

There's no easy way to figure out why people don't always like us. Some of them are just wrapped up in their own world. Others have silly judgments or prejudices that run like fences five miles high, that they aren't going to climb anytime soon. All you can do is do your best to be a friend to the people that you empathize with and that also empathize with you. That last part is really important.

I spent a long time of my life trying to make friends with people that were full of sarcasm. These people were quick to make rude comments about others, whether it be famous people or even close friends and family. I felt some sort of approval because I was included in these little inside sly statements without, for once in my life, being the target of them. It made me proud. At least for a little while. It's that vague sense of approval that was giving me the false sense of having true friendships. The reality was that I was just waiting my turn in line to be the next one that my alleged friends were going to turn on.

Looking back, those friends never bothered to really get to know me. As much time as we spent together, they barely knew a thing about me. Nowadays I have learned that I need to make friendships with people that actually take the time to listen to me and truly care, and then I need to return the favor. This is something that you will learn too.

Listen to Your Gut

If you play close attention when you are with somebody, even if you are just getting to know them for the first time, you will get some sort of signal as to whether you feel comfortable opening up to them or if they are someone that isn't worthy of your attention. Although your gut feeling might be totally wrong and you should not judge them, you are free to decide whether you want to keep hanging out with them.

It's easy to get wrapped up in the social aspects of how everyone is reacting. The older we get the less we open up to people and the more we feel it is socially acceptable to withhold being an honest and sincere person. Just because that is the way others are acting doesn't mean that's the way you have to carry yourself.

Sure maybe the majority of them won't like you. But that's when you have to remind yourself that it's not really you that they don't like. It is the person that they think you are they don't like. Is it worth your time to try to change their mind about who you really are? 99 out of 100 times, the answer is No. Unless you've got the hots for them.

People are too consumed in the system of seeking approval and worried about what everybody else thinks, just like you are right now. You don't have the time to get to know somebody when you just met them, yet, you will be making a decision on the spot - like, or not like. If you do it to them, then you shouldn't mind when they do it to you.

There may also be that one person in the room that was captivated by you. Your next soulmate could be right there. But you and they aren't going to know that until you open up and let your soul shine. Don't be a robot. Don't worry if they like you or not. Be true to yourself the rest will fall into place.

How Do I Know What They Really Think?

There is a fine line between respecting somebody's opinion and being a complete doormat for trying to do whatever it takes to please them. Let's weigh in on the side that you are simply trying to be respectful. Let's say for example that you are thinking about your significant other's parents, or perhaps somebody on a professional level. There are times in life when knowing what the other person thinks of us is actually useful. It's not that we are trying to change the way we are, it's just that we respect their opinion and would like to know. We also like opening cans of worms apparently.

A Double-Edged Sword

Don't worry we all do it. But what sort of answers are we really looking for? It's not like we are going to get any information that is going to matter. At least nothing that we cannot give to ourselves. There's an old saying by Bette Davis that is: "What other people think of me is none of my business." That quote definitely applies when dealing with somebody you respect. If you were to suddenly ask them what they thought about you then you could quickly deplete any amount of respect that the person has for you.

In these situations, the only thing you should do is accept the fact that the person has you in their life. Enjoy the short time that you get to spend in each

9

other's company and move on from there. You really have no business knowing what somebody thinks of you anyhow. Doesn't it just pull you away from being the person that you truly are? Imagine if suddenly they said something like, "Well you're great but your laughter is annoying." Do you think you would ever laugh quite the same around that person again? Probably not.

If you had never asked they probably would have never told you and they would have just put up with the fact that they had a distaste for your nasal propensities when belting out a good ole belly laughter. No matter what people think about one person or another, it usually boils down to one of two outcomes: they either accept you for who you are, or they move on.

Some people in life will stick around and do their best to try and manipulate you into fitting into their standardized mold. They are sociopaths. Using others to simply get what they want. That's why they will manipulate you. Avoid these people at all costs.

Close Attention Will Cue You In

If you want to know what somebody thinks of you pay attention to the little things that they do. Everyone has their own unique language of being able to reach out to other people. Not everyone is going to pull you aside and say "Gee I think you're swell." They might just spend some time sitting quietly with you. But you know, they could be sitting with somebody else and instead they chose you.

Some people out there make it really hard to believe them when it comes to their devotion and friendship. They are stoic and reserved, maybe rough around the edges. Maybe they speak with aggression. The truth is that hard-edged attitude is nothing more than a cover-up. Don't buy into it.

At the same time if you find yourself being put on the line emotionally or mentally, let alone physically, then simply let the person go. Most of the time people don't change. But if it's somebody that you have to be around, like an in-law, then you will have to find a way to put up with them and what they think of you, at least for your spouse's sake. Hold your head up high and stay confident.

They say that we can choose our friends, but we can't choose our family. So why would you have to bend over backward to be somebody else just because a stranger else doesn't like you? Don't make them your friend, and they won't make you either.

When it comes to family, it's is different. Even though you care about them, or at the very least you are tied to them, it doesn't mean that you have to be somebody else in their presence just so that they can like you. You're certainly not respecting them, or yourself if you do that.

Stand tall and remember, they probably aren't thinking about you anyhow. If they are, and it's that important, they will let you know one way or another.

Are You a Brand?

If you're a brand or aspiring to become a brand, then wondering what other people think of you takes on a whole new meaning. It's not like you are running around wondering what people think of you because you necessarily want to please them or seek their approval, it's more likely that you are trying to be self-promoting and even possibly a little bit of a leader in the eyes of those that appreciate and follow you.

Not That Much Fun

Being a brand is certainly not everything it's cracked up to be. Anybody that is a brand knows this. It's really not fun.

When you are a brand you are essentially working for the people. Therefore, what others think of you doesn't just influence your feelings, it can change your livelihood and ability to make an income. There is a certain amount of "don't give a damn" that still applies to not concerning yourself to what others think. Or at least you have to give off the image that you really don't care, even if deep down inside you have changed your whole image just to go along with what your audience wants. It's just part of playing the game (if that's what you want to call it).

If you want to know what people think about you the best way is simply to interact directly with them. No matter where you are in your career there are always places and opportunities to get to know people on a level completely separate from who you are as a brand. If you are very concerned the internet makes for wonderful opportunities to talk to people without having to fully disclose who you are. People can be quick to flattery even if all they've been tweeting is horrible negative things. When they meet you face-to-face it always seems to be a different story. Then suddenly they are enamored. It's part of the cost of being in the public. Which basically leaves you right back to square one of having to not really give a damn.

Think Ahead and Listen Deeply

If you are a brand you need to anticipate what others think of you. Then based on that anticipation you can grow your image and adjust accordingly. Often times people either don't know what they want until it's right in front of them, or they want the exact same thing that they've had dozens of times before just slightly different. People, as consumers, don't stray too far from their own definition of normal. This can be helpful when you are a brand and try to discover what people think of your brand.

The easiest way to find out is to listen to what people are saying. Listen to your close friends. The ones that are giving you constructive criticism and not the ones that are simply telling you that you are great all the time. Everyone likes compliments, but there comes a point when you are in the business that you really need somebody to lay things down for you on the table.

Find the people in your life that will do this for you and keep them in your life. They are not only real friend, they are also invaluable assets.

Thinking Less Doing More

Thinking less of what others think of you, and do more stuff that you enjoy. If becoming more social is something that you want then you have to throw yourself into situations that require you to be social. For some of us going to the library is a social event. But that's probably not enough to get you out of your shell and get you interacting with people.

Don't Wait

Whatever it is that you want to do, just go ahead and do it. You don't need to wait to have the approval of others before you follow your dreams. If you wait around for their approval, you are liable to never even get it. For worse, if you do eventually get the approval you seek, you could miss out on your opportunity to follow your dream and nothing is quite as biting.

There will be moments throughout your life that you will slip back into that frontier of wondering about your self-image. Thankfully those moments will not last nearly as long as they once did, and they certainly won't be as crippling as they were before. The more you begin to realize that we are all in this together, the more these concerns about what other people think will start to fall away.

It's like the way a snake sheds its skin. The old skin is completely useless now. Just keep pushing through worrying and step into a new mode full of confidence and action. You will find that when you start acting in a manner that is true to yourself, every aspect of who you are takes on an important quality. That quality not only nurtures how you feel throughout the day, but it also acts like a mirror and reflects back to other people those qualities that they have dormant.

Now Look at You

When you stop worrying about how people think of you, you will start helping others recognize the best in themselves. And guess what. They will love you for that. That's right – the best way to get people to like you is to actually care less about how they think of you, and make them feel good about how you think of them.

People are continually on the lookout for win/win situations. As you push yourself into this arena and mode of thinking you will fall back on your ability to succeed as opposed to seeking outside approval to build your confidence.

People find this drive through all sorts of different methods. There's no exact way that is going to get you to suddenly start being confident. For a lot of people, it's all about setting small goals that lead up to one really big accomplishment that they have always dreamed of. You work on it just a little bit at a time and before you know it you arrive at your goal. Once you get a taste of that victory there is no turning back.

Learning to Not Care

So what does it mean to not care? What does it feel like to really not concern yourself with what others think of you? Imagine it for a moment. Seriously. Take a second right now and see yourself as the kind of person that doesn't stop for one second to even consider anybody else's opinion. What did you see yourself doing? Were you dressed differently? Carrying yourself differently? How is that different than the person you are right now?

Get to Moving

Whatever differences you saw are exactly the sort of things that you need to work on changing immediately. Don't let the things that are holding you back continue to do so any longer. Whether it's fear of not having the financial security that you now have, or maybe you are scared of being alone and don't want to leave an unfulfilling relationship. Whatever it is that is keeping you back, don't let that fear control you.

Instead start to use that fear as a compass to guide you in the direction of the changes that you need to make in your life right now. Starting today. Remember it's all about making baby steps. You don't wake up one day as an infant and start sprinting around the house. You have to learn to stand first, then you walk, one step at a time. The big change that you have to make in your life, away from caring what other people think, can be done at your own rate.

Some people go blazing into their future leaving behind a complete lifetime of unease and settling, only to be met with a crash of reality when they finally realize that they didn't really think everything through all the way. For others, there never is a crash. They just keep soaring forward closer to the dreams that they have. I would wage it best to weigh in on the safe side and take carefully thought-out steps. Not for the concerns of others, but for the concern of your own emotional and mental wellbeing.

It's Quite a Shift

Going from a life of living for everyone else, to a life where you are suddenly putting yourself first can leave you a little angry and disgruntled for the people that you changed for. The truth is, though, you can't take it out on them, or even yourself. It just simply is a matter of fact. If you think about in the sense that you have evolved, you can start to see that in many ways you are no longer the person that you once were.

That means that the way that you interact now with those in your life isn't the same as it once was. You will not be able to have the same relationships that you once did. The glue that held them together will not be there anymore. This is okay. It's nothing to get frustrated about and if you try to keep a relationship or friendship together only because you were once super close, you will learn eventually that things change.

All that matters is that you don't burn any bridges today or tomorrow or anytime for that matter. You never know what tomorrow brings. In the meantime, all you can do is focus on not caring about what others think so much today. That means that every time you find yourself stressing out about things like your appearance, or whether somebody liked what you said or not, you have to actively learn to shrug it off.

Where Are You

If you catch yourself thinking too much again, take a deep breath and ask yourself, "Where am I in all of this?"

Sometimes we have to be around people that we really don't like or that make us feel uncomfortable. It's just one of those cold hard facts of life. It happens in the professional sphere all the time. All you can do is remind yourself of your role in the project and let things slide off your back. There is no use letting them get the most of you.

When you stop and think about it there are only 24 hours in each day. That means that you only have so much time for thoughts, hopes, desires, concerns, and you only have so much time to act upon them. Reminding yourself that your time is limited can help you realize that when you start letting somebody else consume all of your thinking, you may be wasting your life.

Take Back Your Life

Start taking back your life by controlling these thoughts as they come up. Sometimes they may seem like a snowball coming down the side of a mountain and before you know it they are much larger than you ever expected.

When you sit and think about what people said or what they might have thought, you are living in the past and wasting the moment that is now. When the snowball finally hits, there isn't any substance to it. You can worry your entire life away but that won't change a thing and it won't make you a better person either.

Instead of spending all that time wondering what others think of you, you could take back your life and start doing the things you enjoy. Even better, you can start exploring new things. If you are open to possibilities, the world is your oyster as they say. Don't waste your time worrying about what the oyster thinks as you crack it open to find your pearl.

Stand strong against the tide of those that try to tell you how to be and who to be. It will infect your ability to listen to your own intuition if you let it. You can cure it quite simply by letting go of the control you give others over your life. The only person's approval you need is your own. Start making yourself happy and the rest will fall into place.

Conclusion

Wondering what other people think of you is something we all do from time to time. It is the way that you handle it that will make a difference on how much joy and fulfillment that you experience in your life.

If you are spending all of your time running around trying to make everyone happy all of the time, you are leaving little time for your own happiness. You have other things to do with your time. It doesn't mean you are better than anybody else, but it doesn't mean you are worse either.

Win a free

kindle
OASIS

Let us know what you thought of this book to enter the sweepstake at:

http://booksfor.review/peoplethink

Printed in Great Britain
by Amazon